I Can Fix It!

Solving Problems

Sommer Conway

SOCIAL AND EMOTIONAL LEARNING FOR THE REAL WORLD™

Rosen Classroom™

I keep missing the bus!
That's a problem.

What's wrong?
I sleep too late.

What can I do?
I think carefully.

What could happen?
I try to picture it.

I make a choice.
I set an alarm clock.

I can fix the problem!

Words to Know

alarm clock

bus